PENCIL ART Volume One

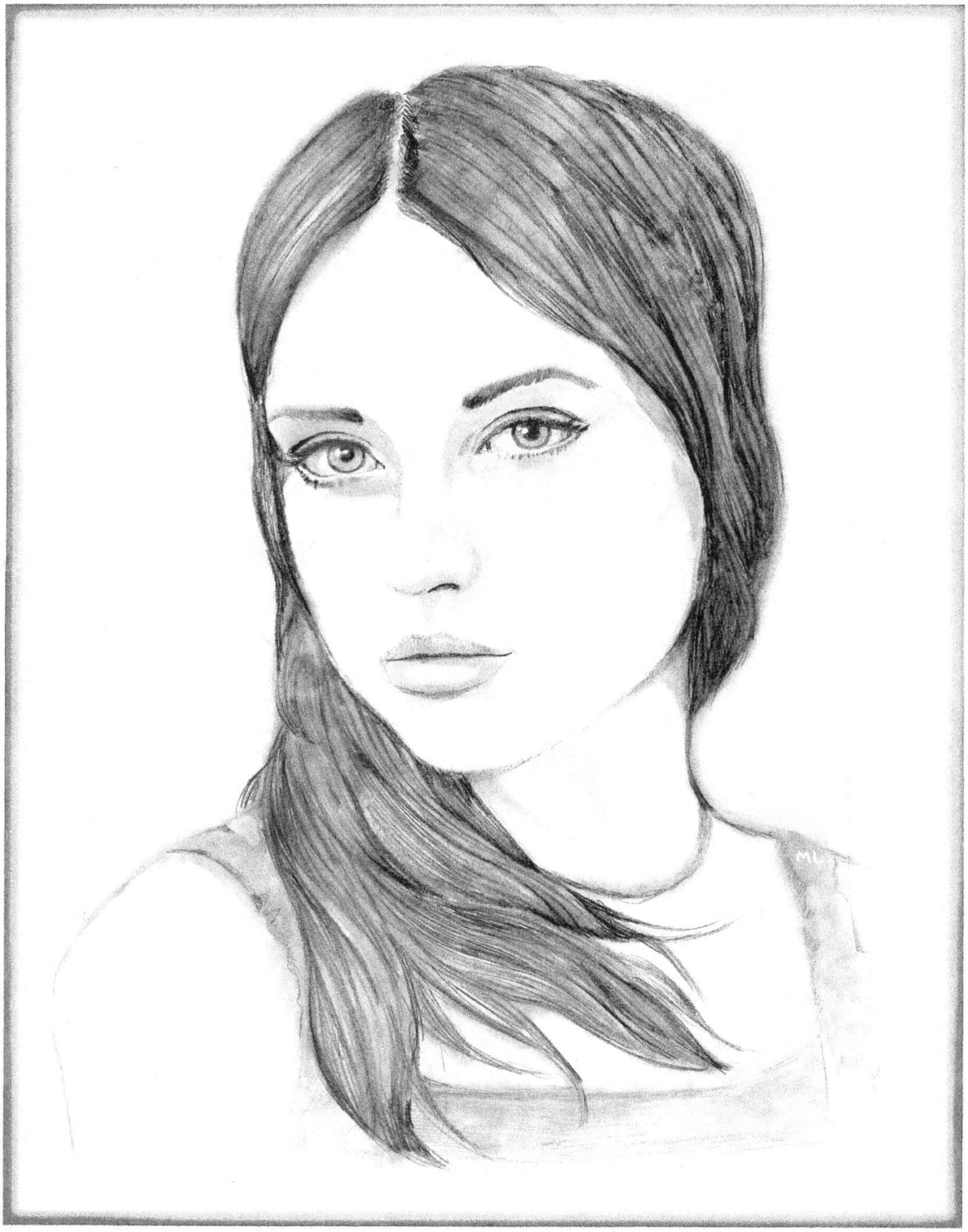

By M. Lovins

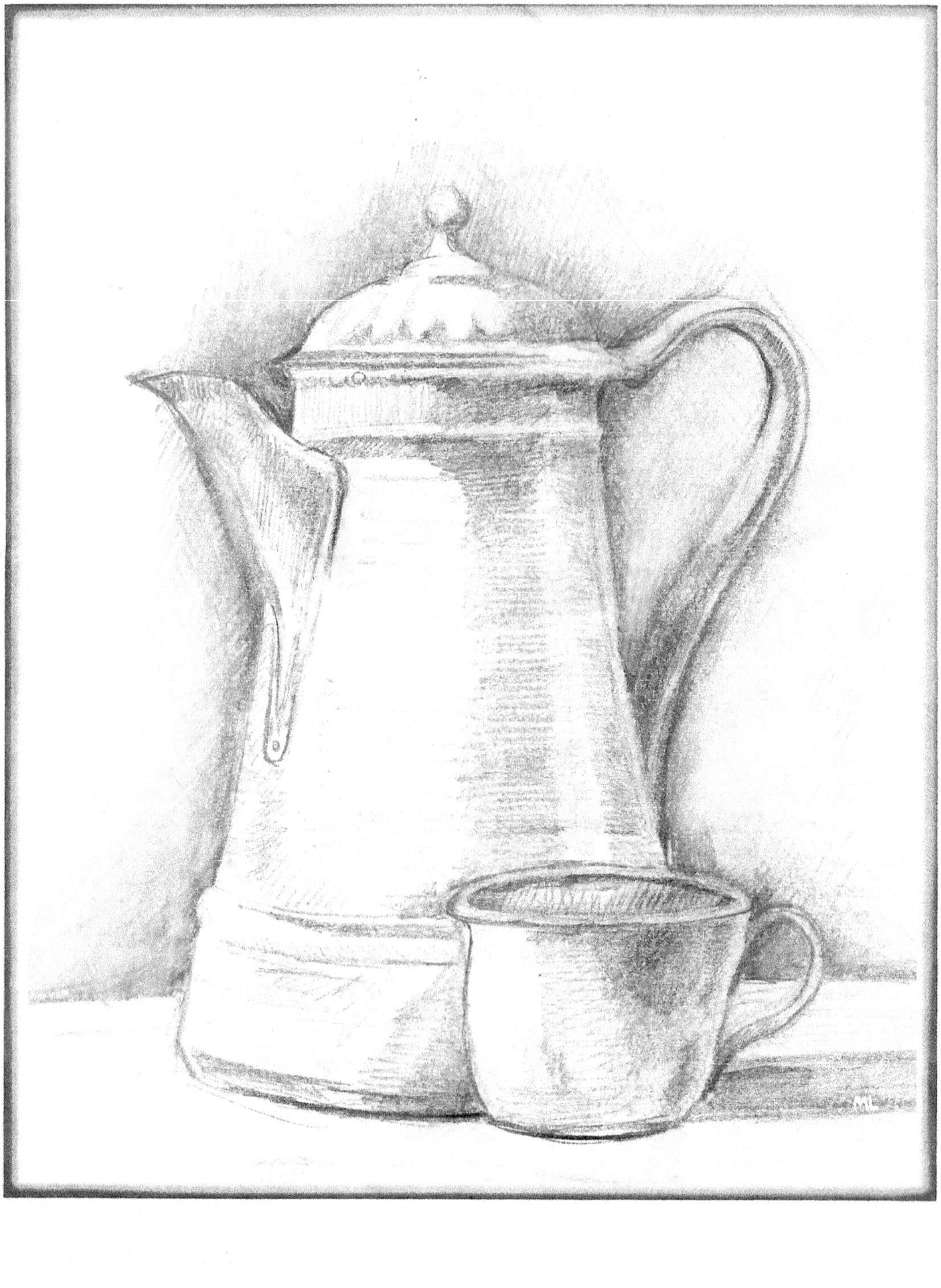

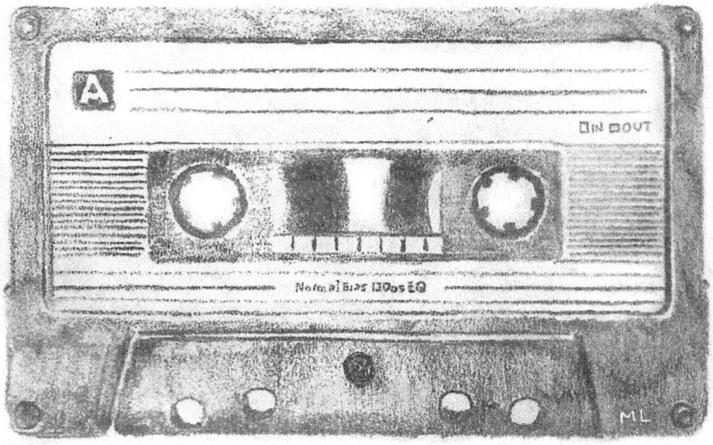
A
IN OUT
Normal Bias 120µs EQ
ML

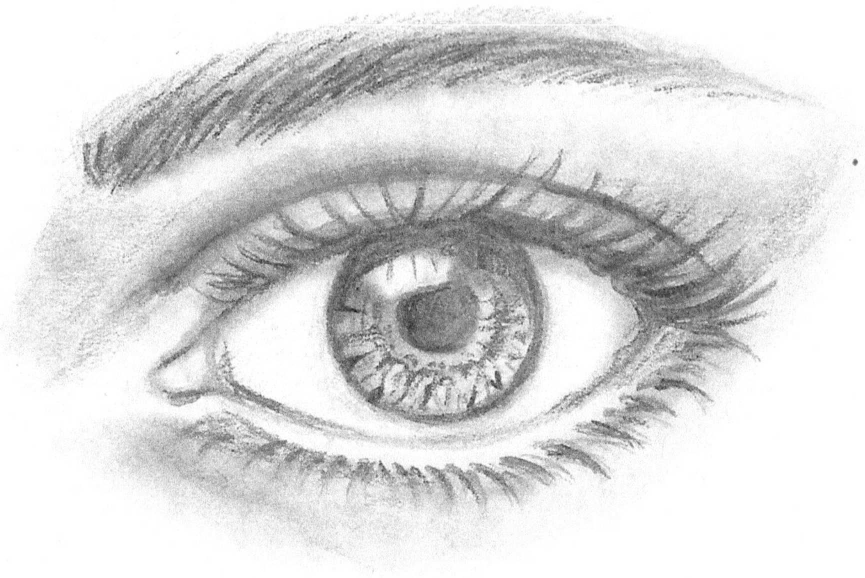

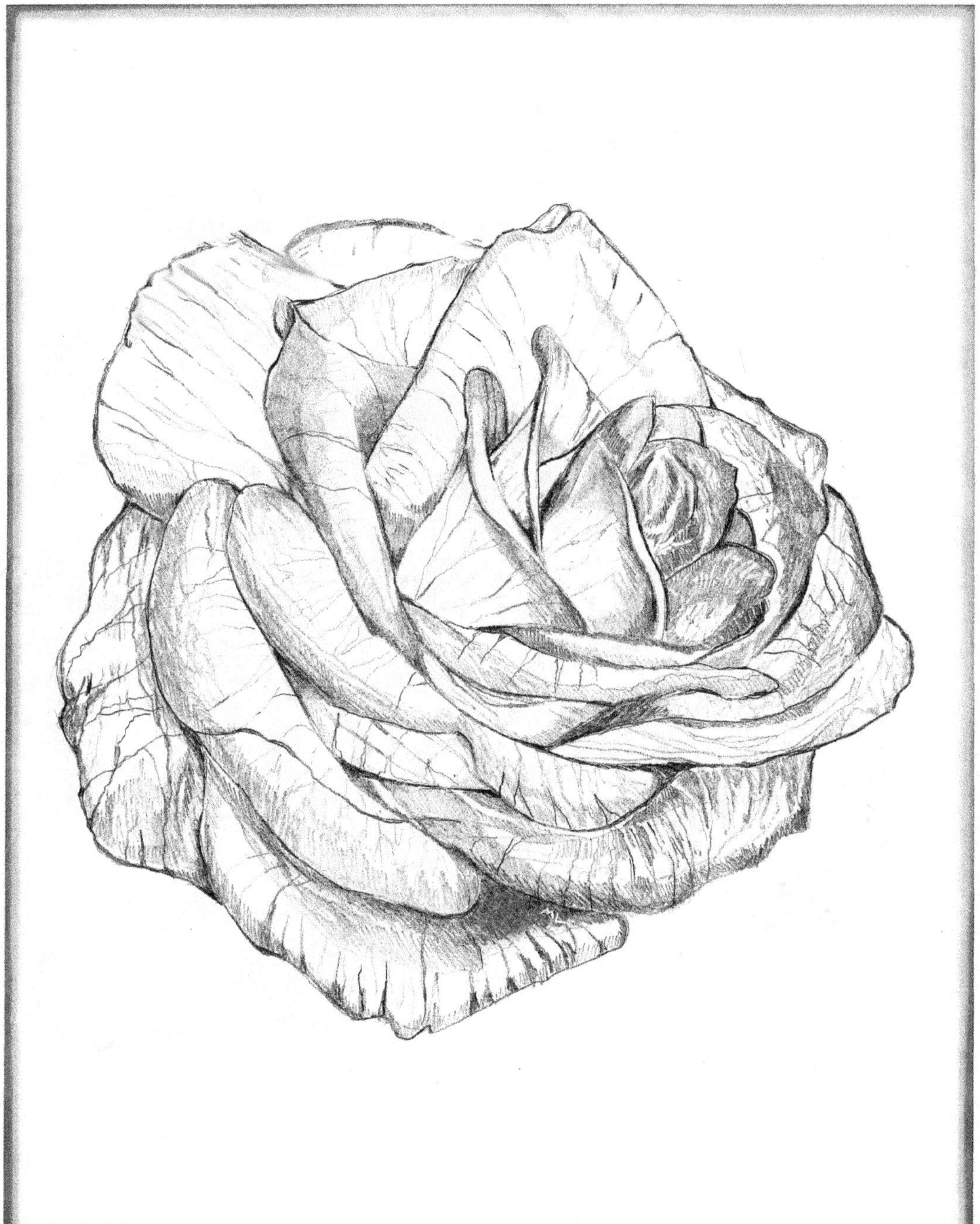

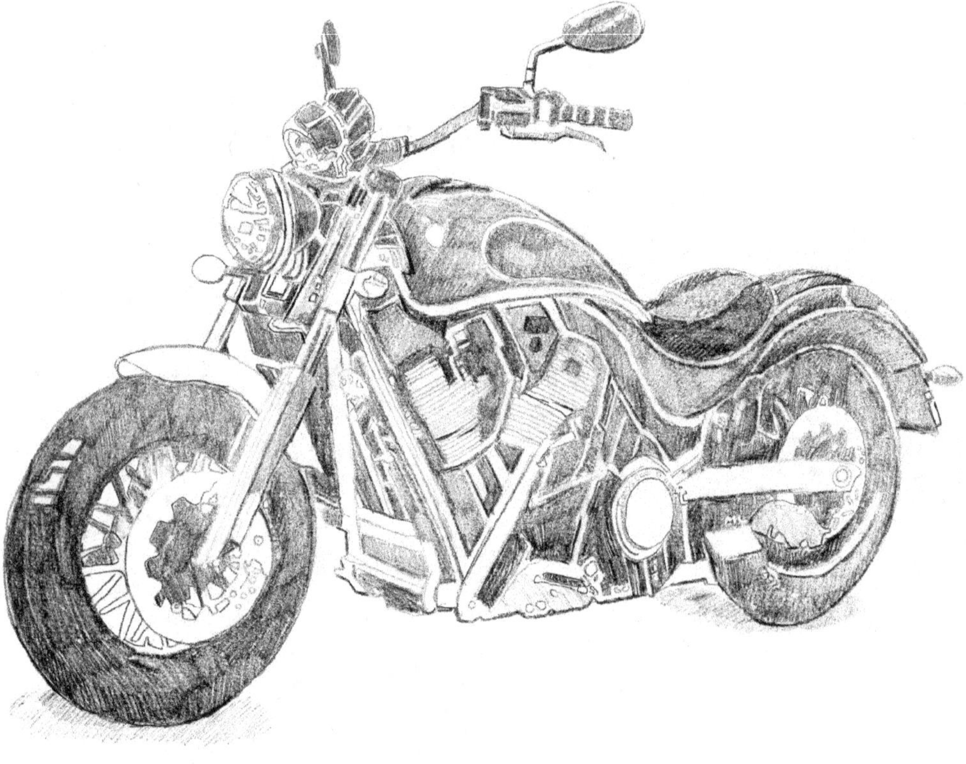

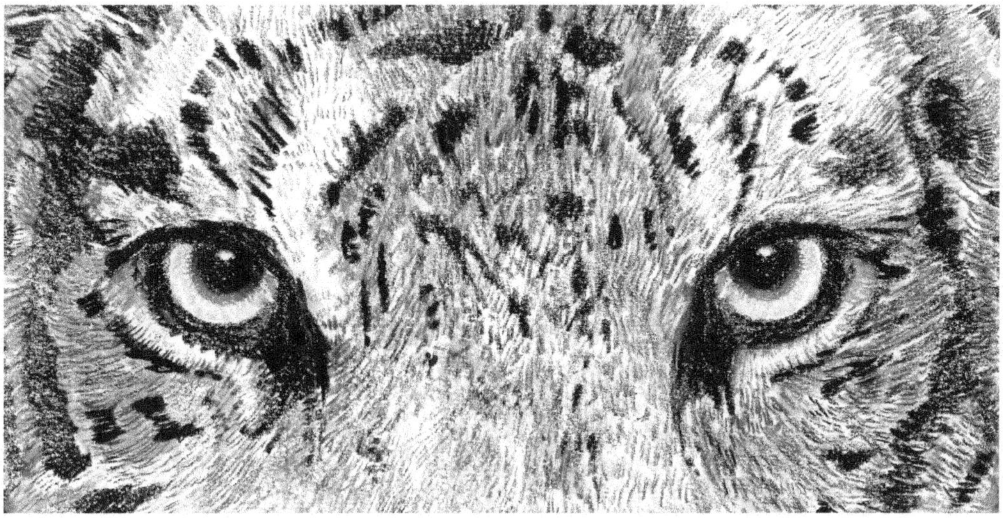

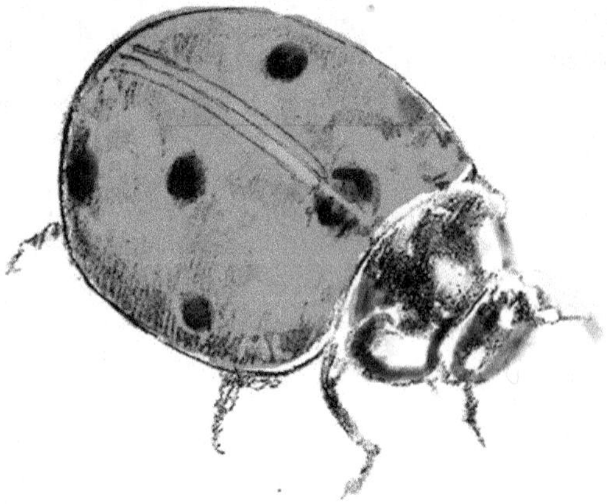

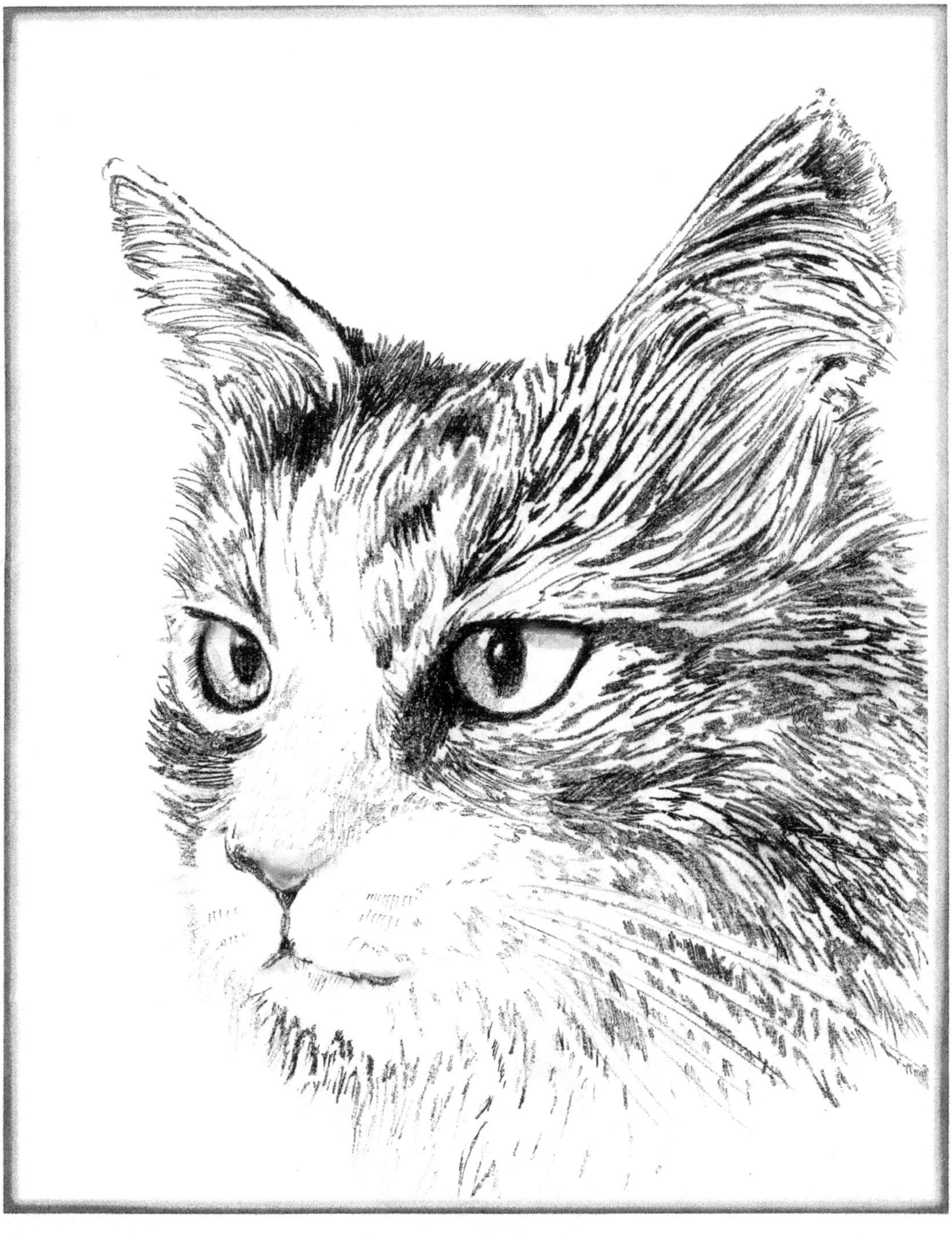

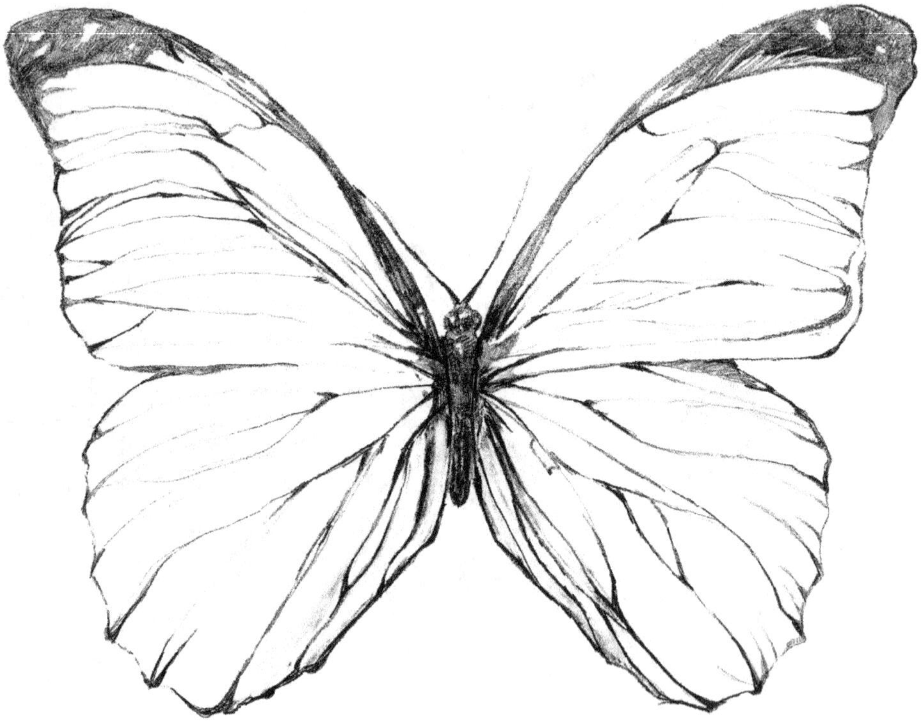

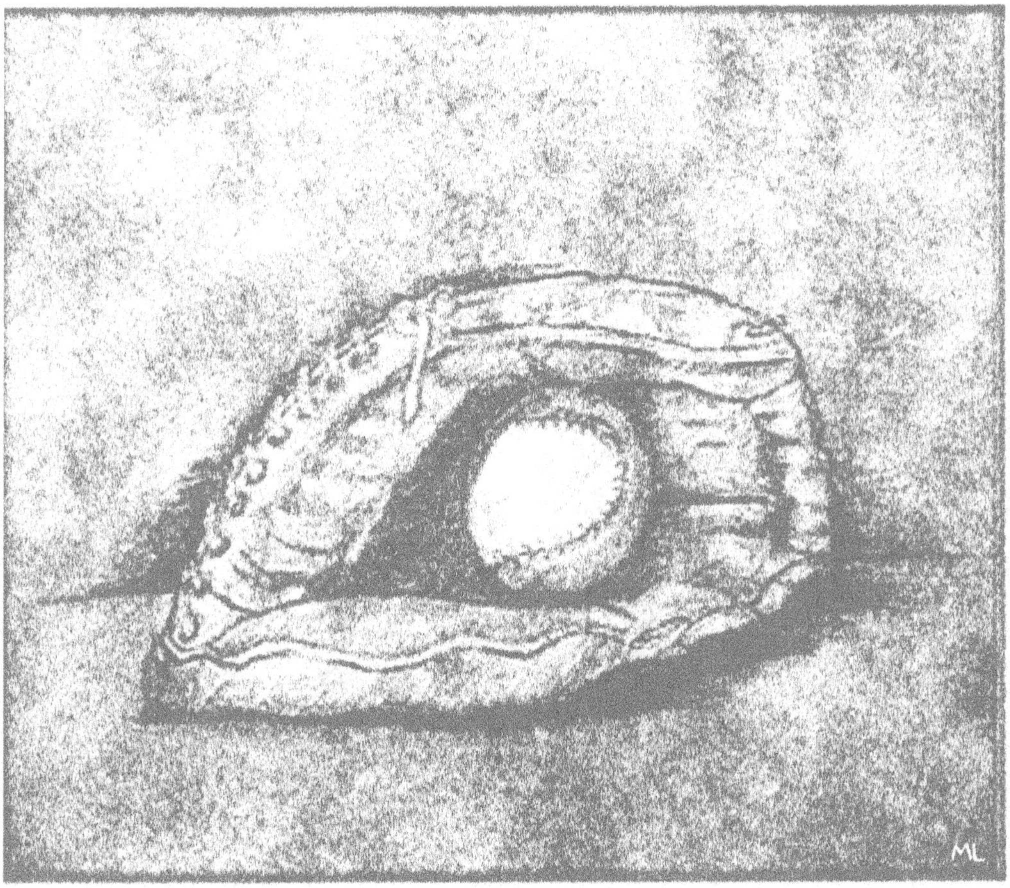
ML

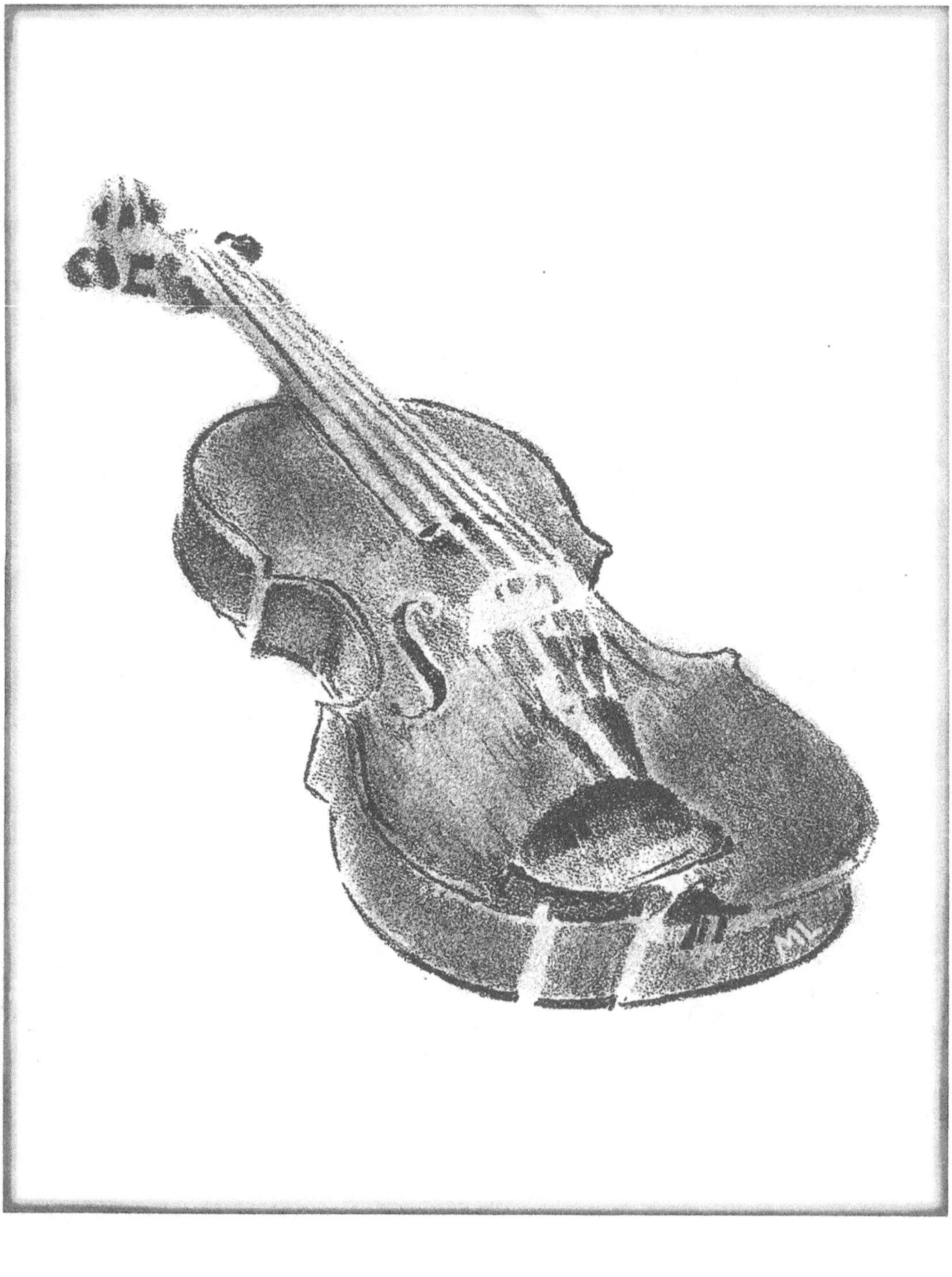
ML

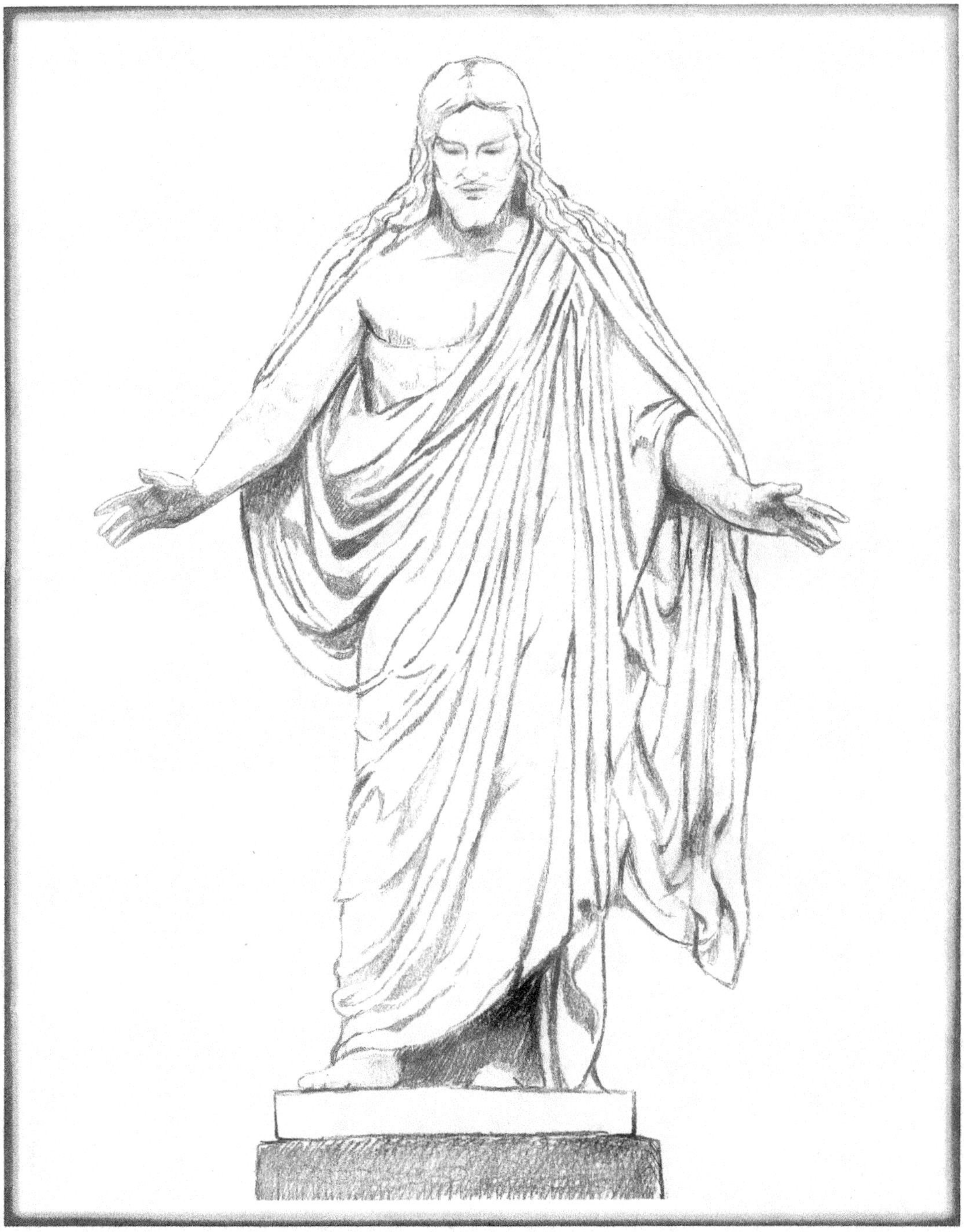

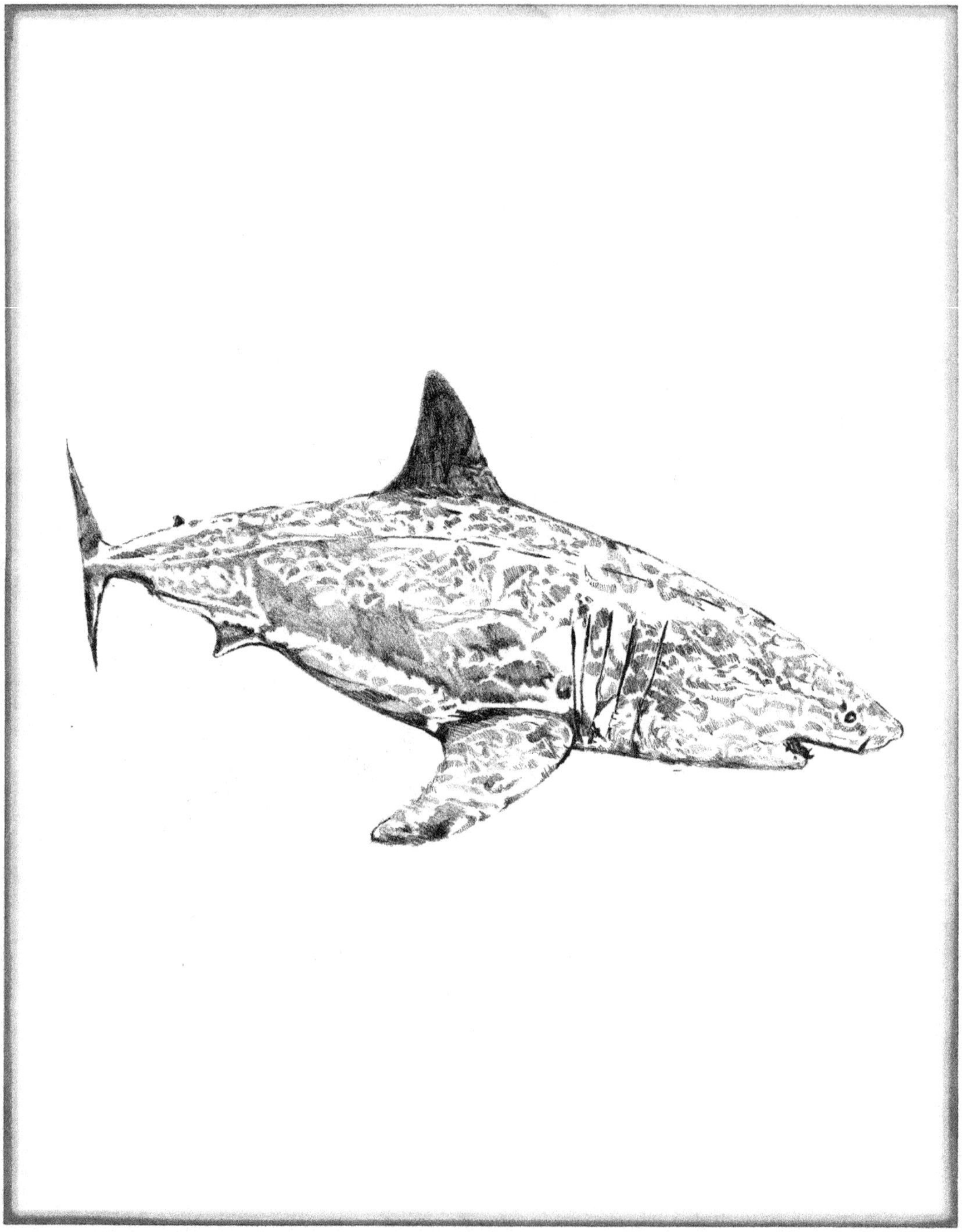

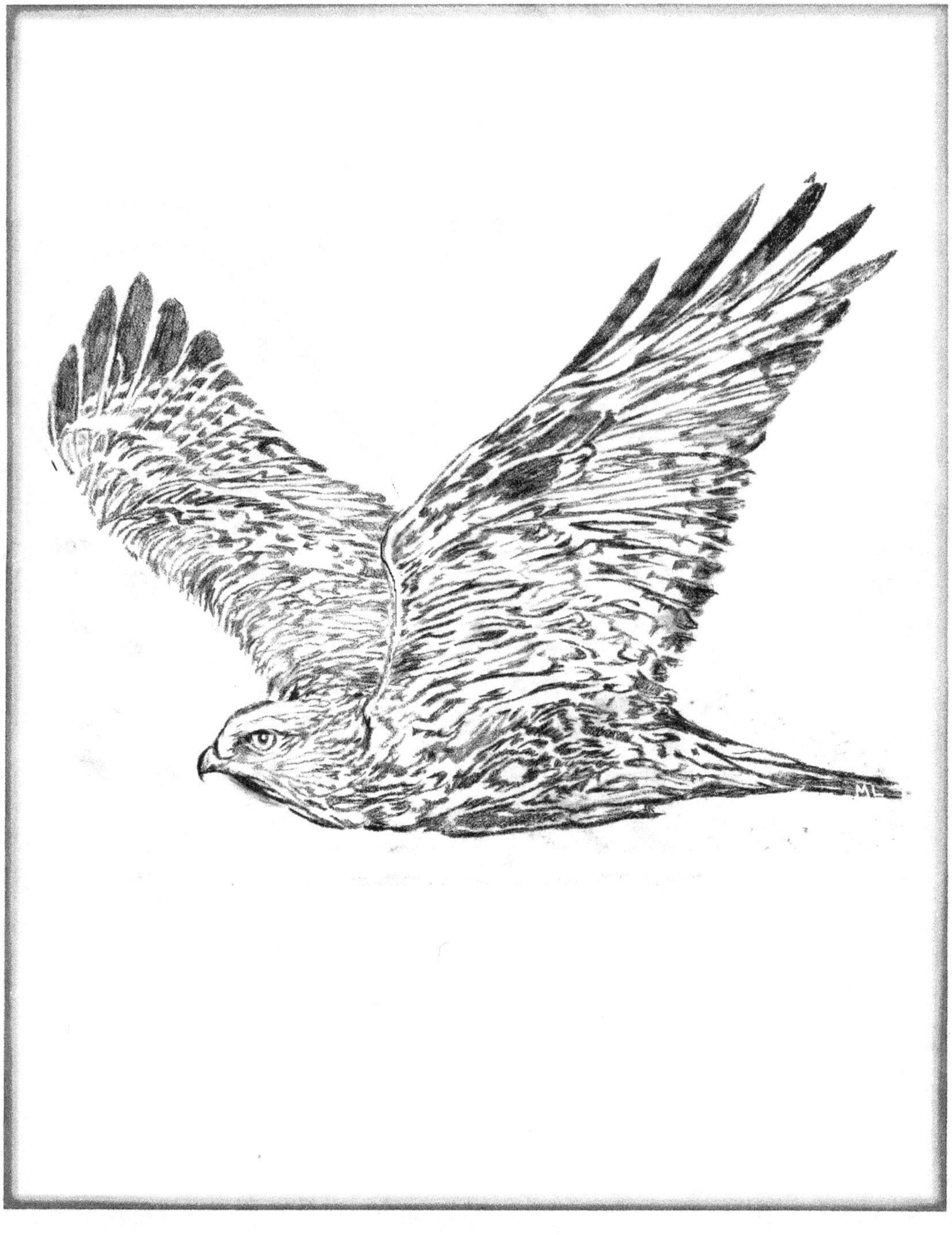
ML

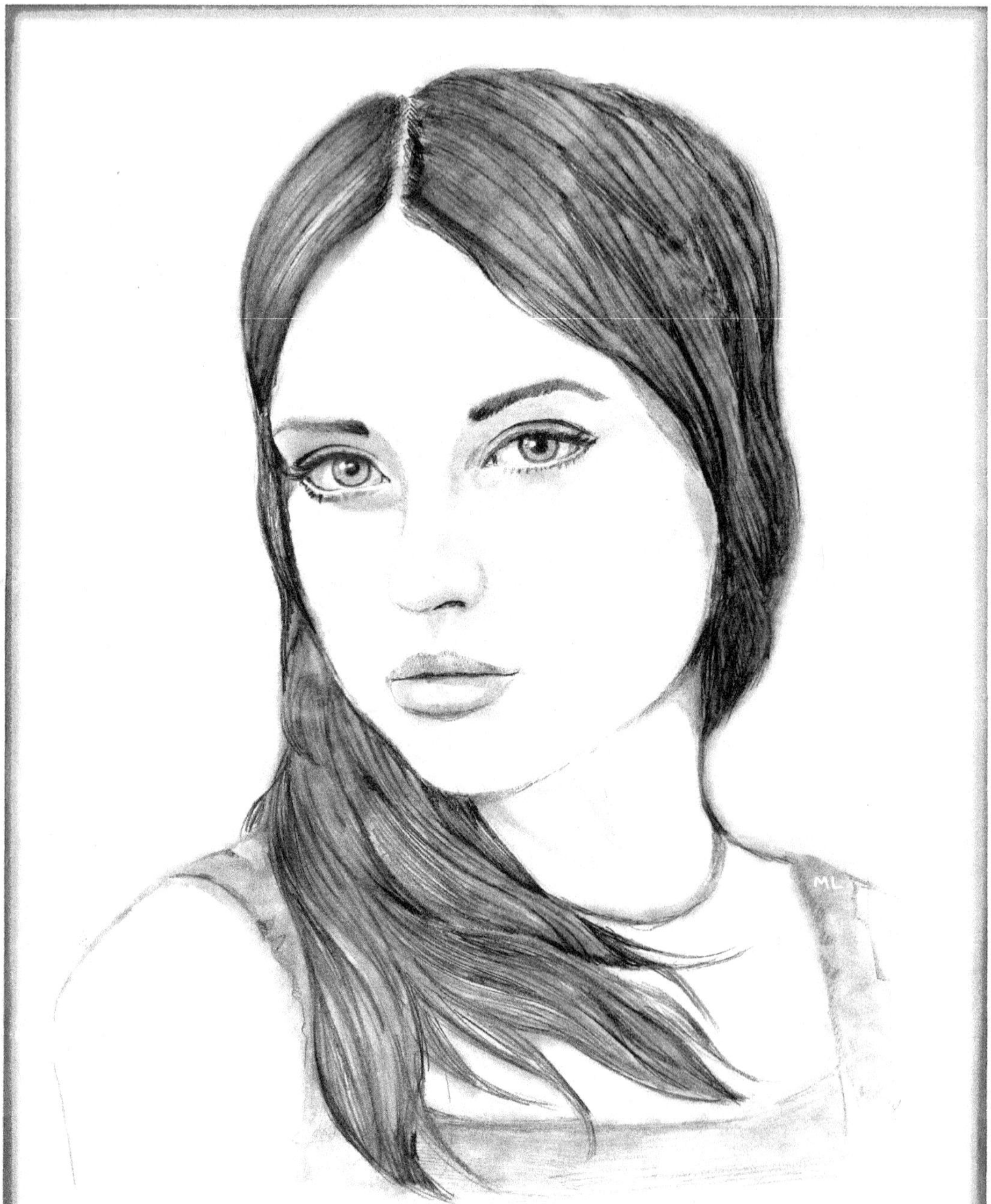
ML

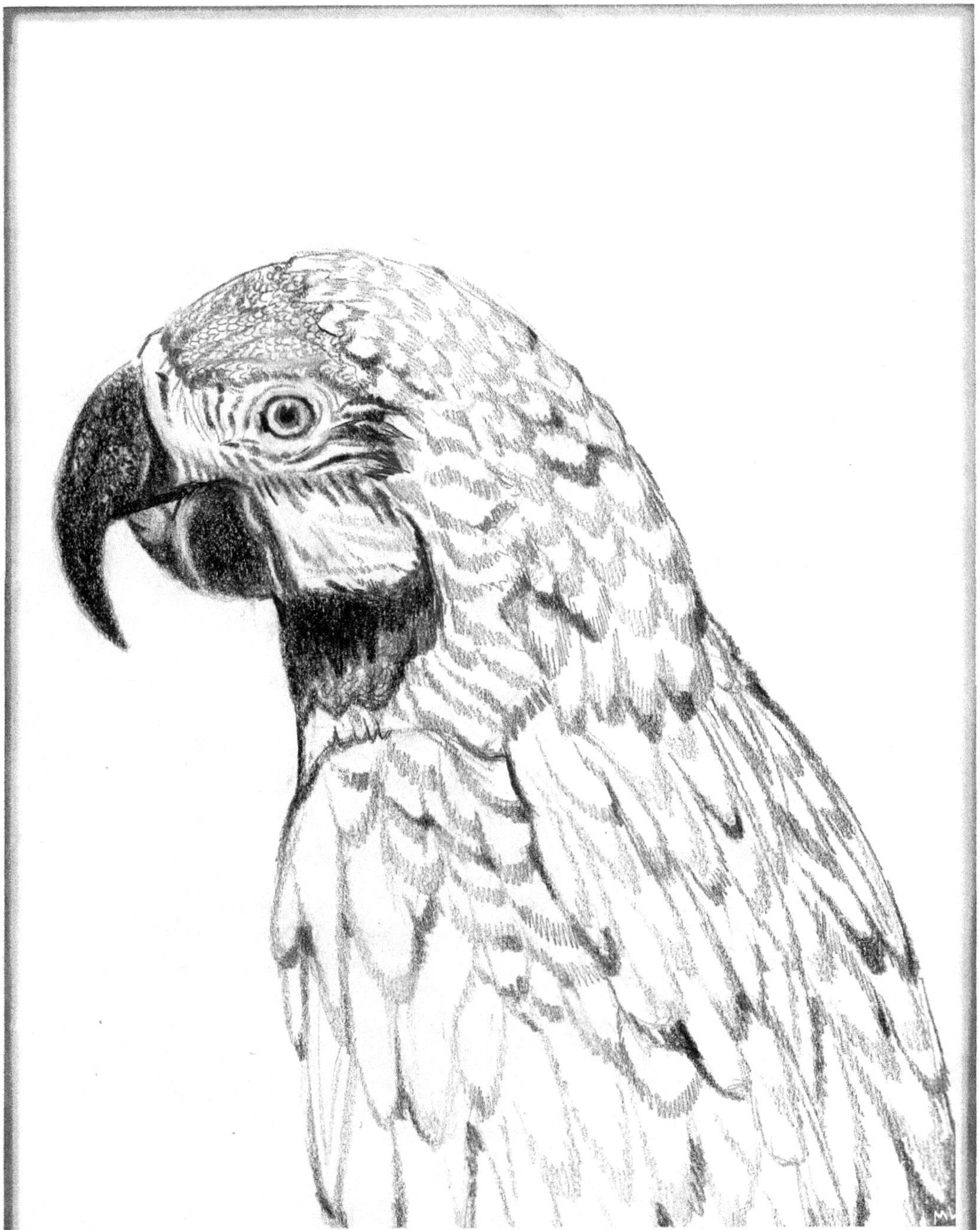

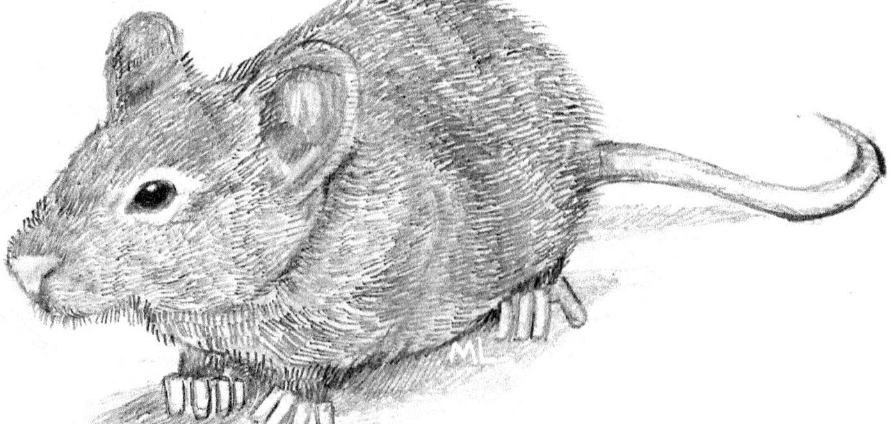

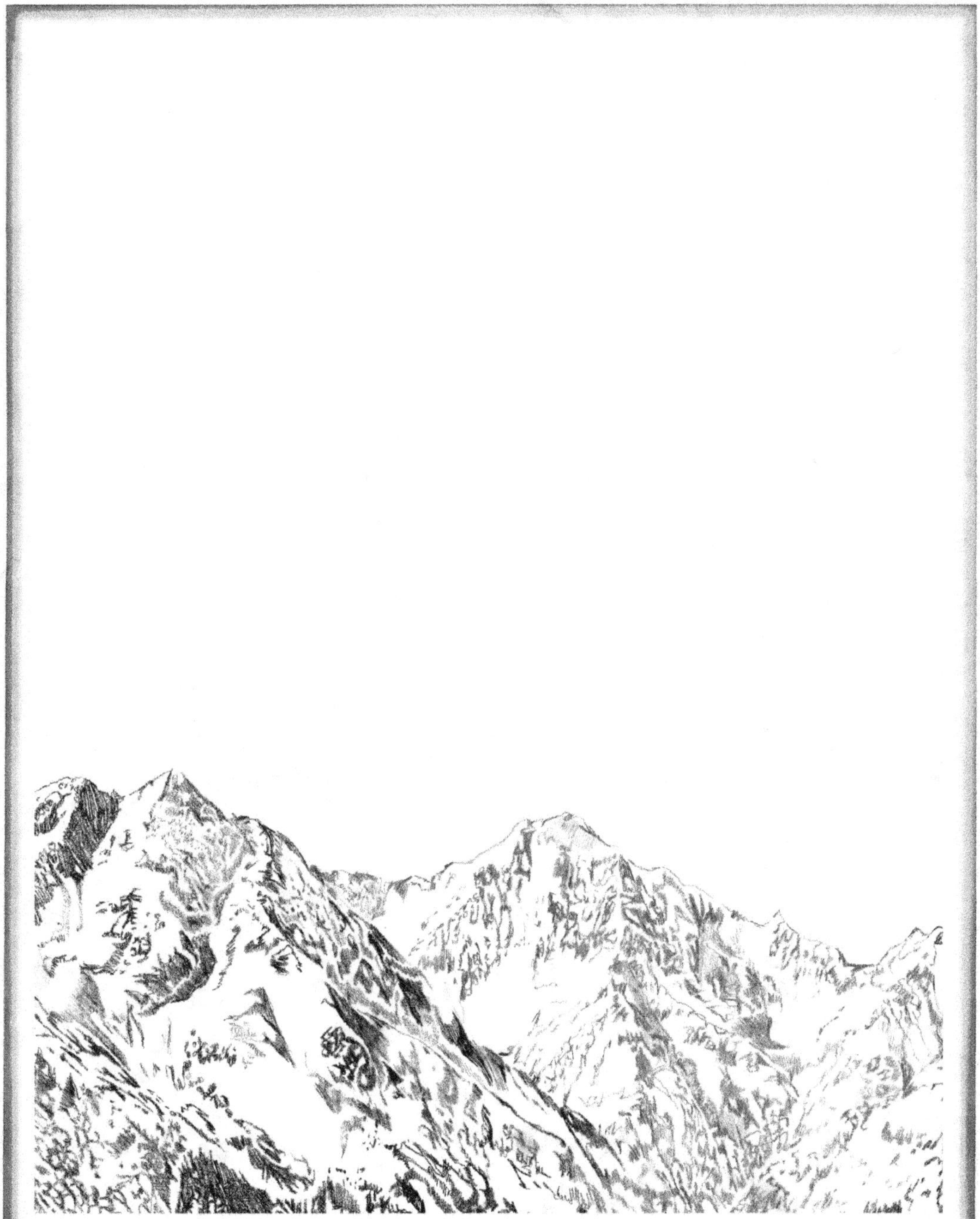

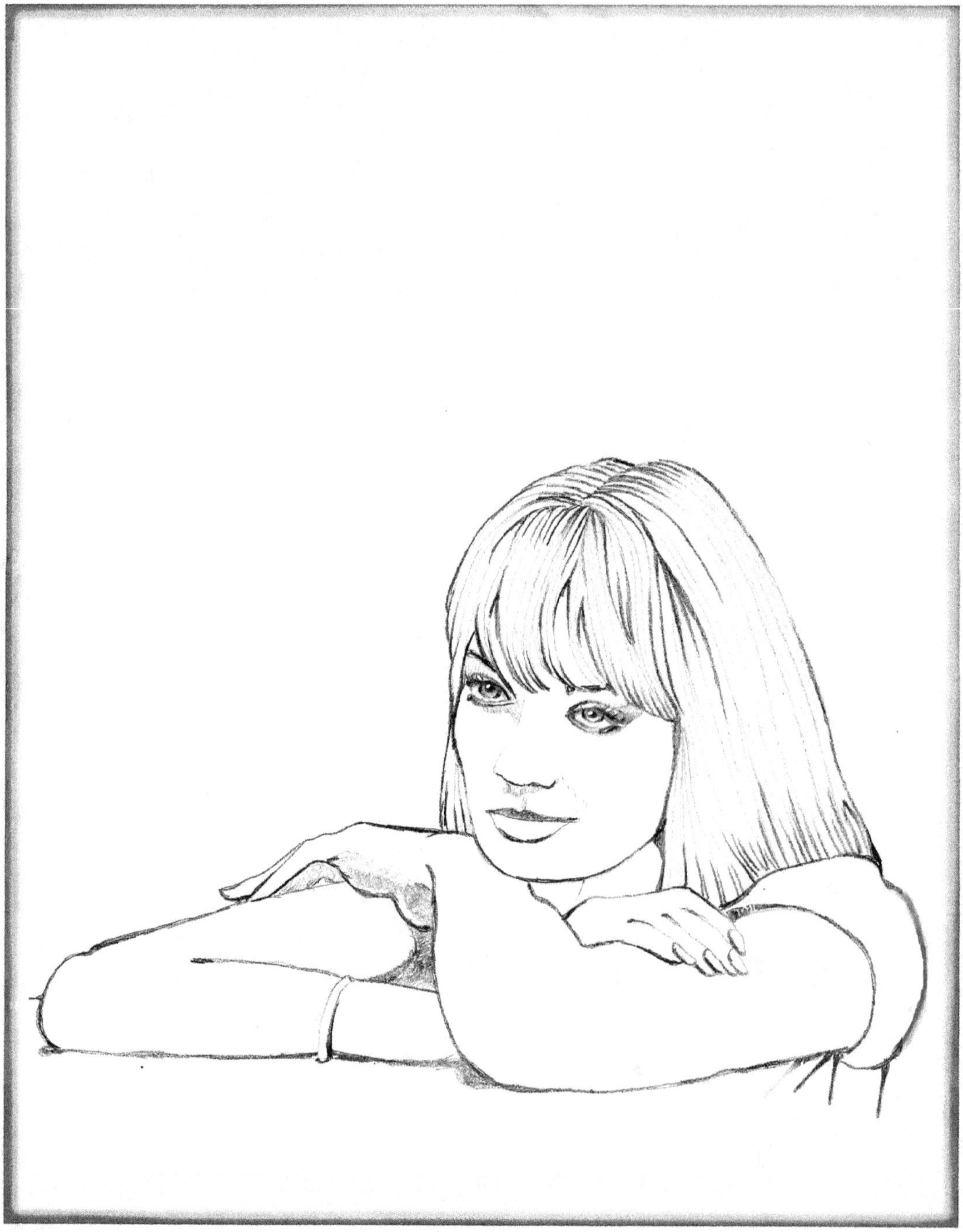

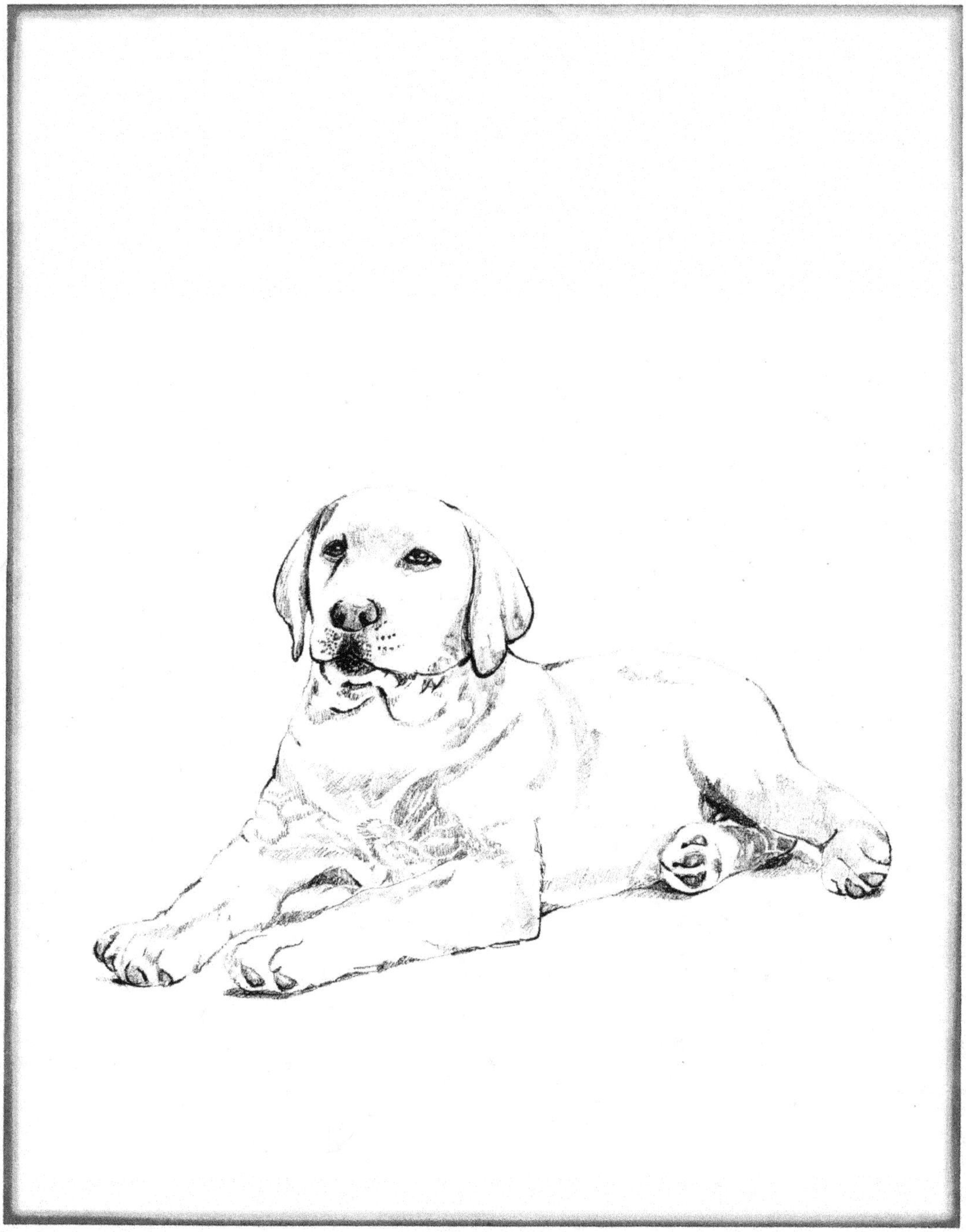

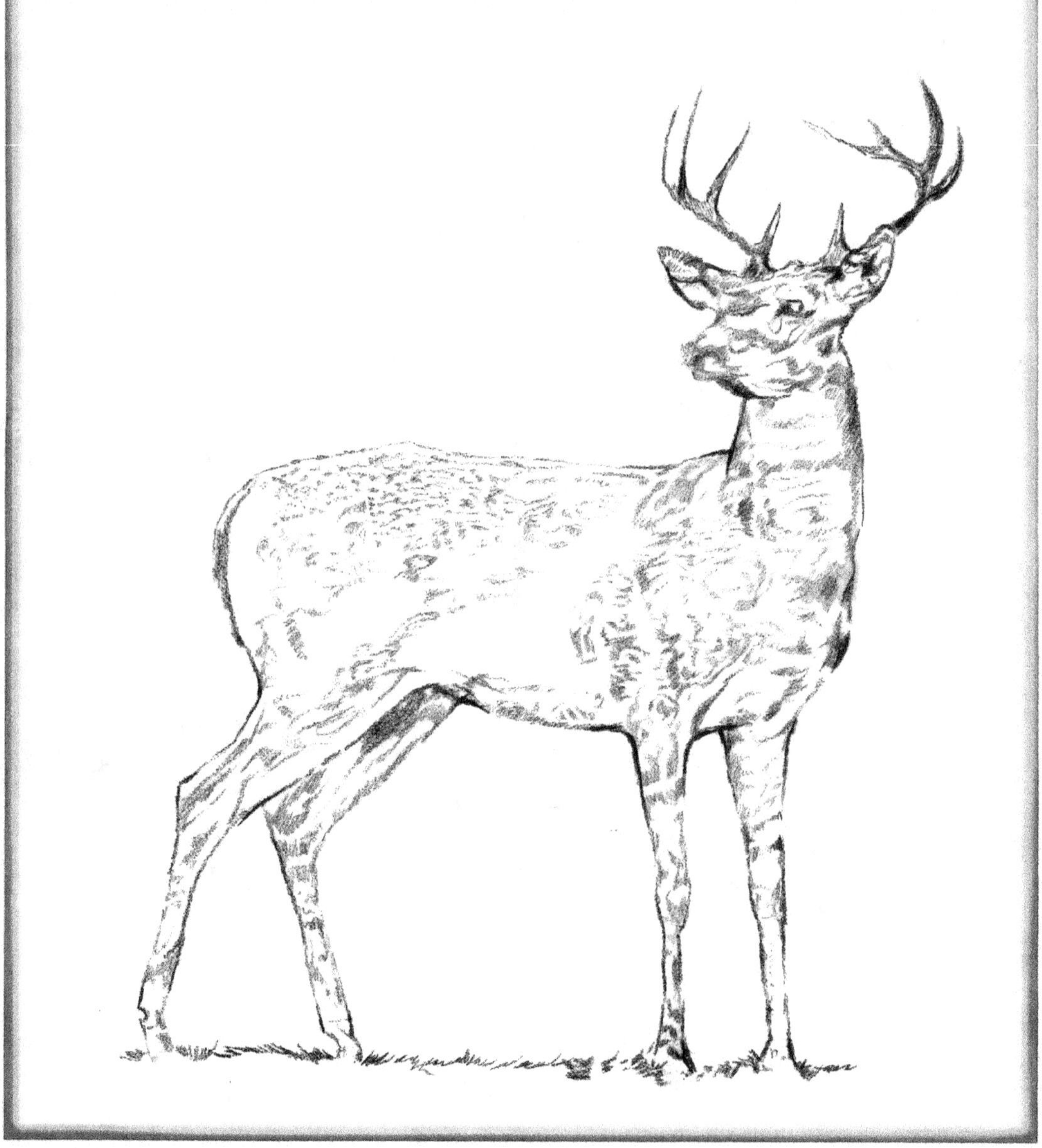

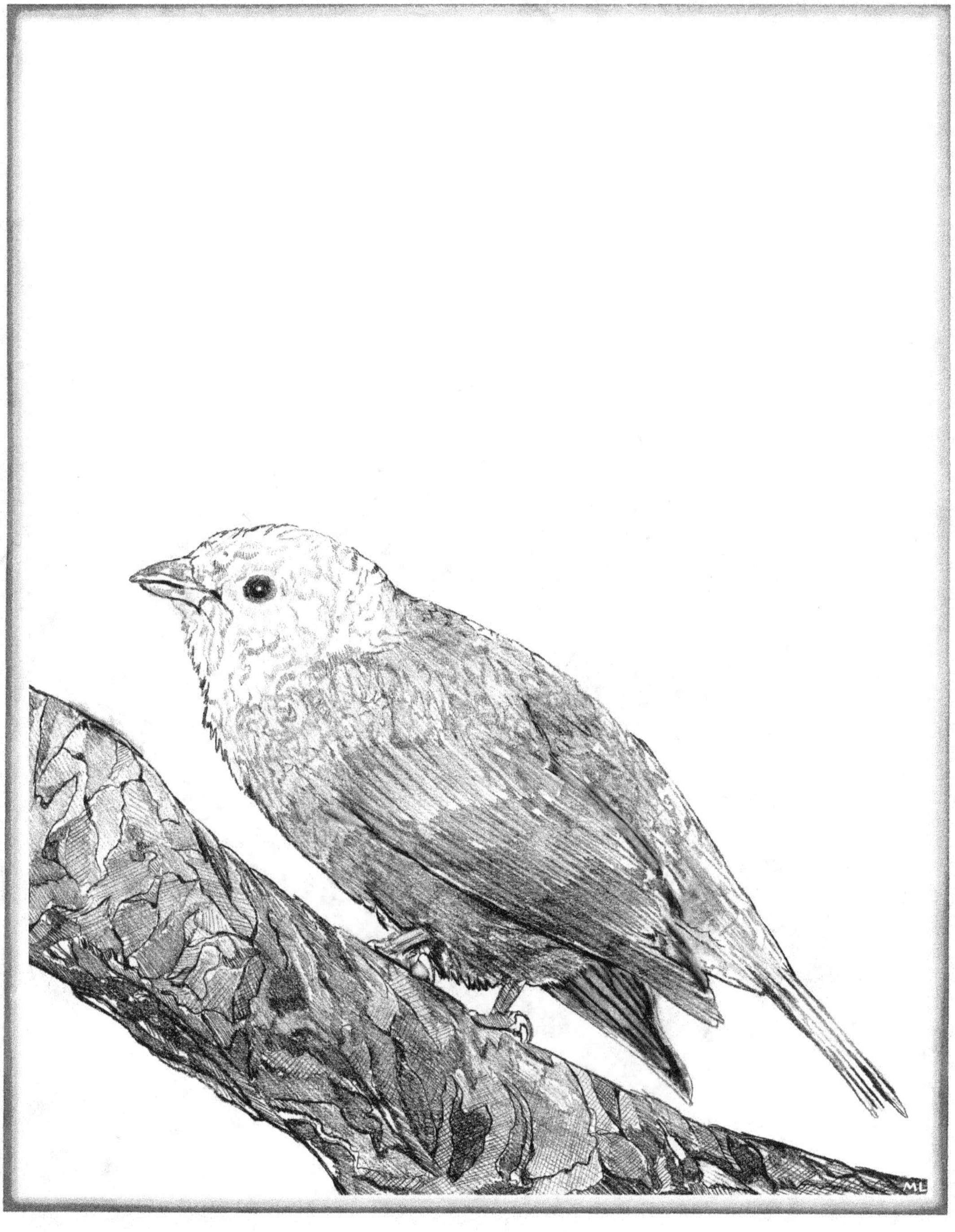

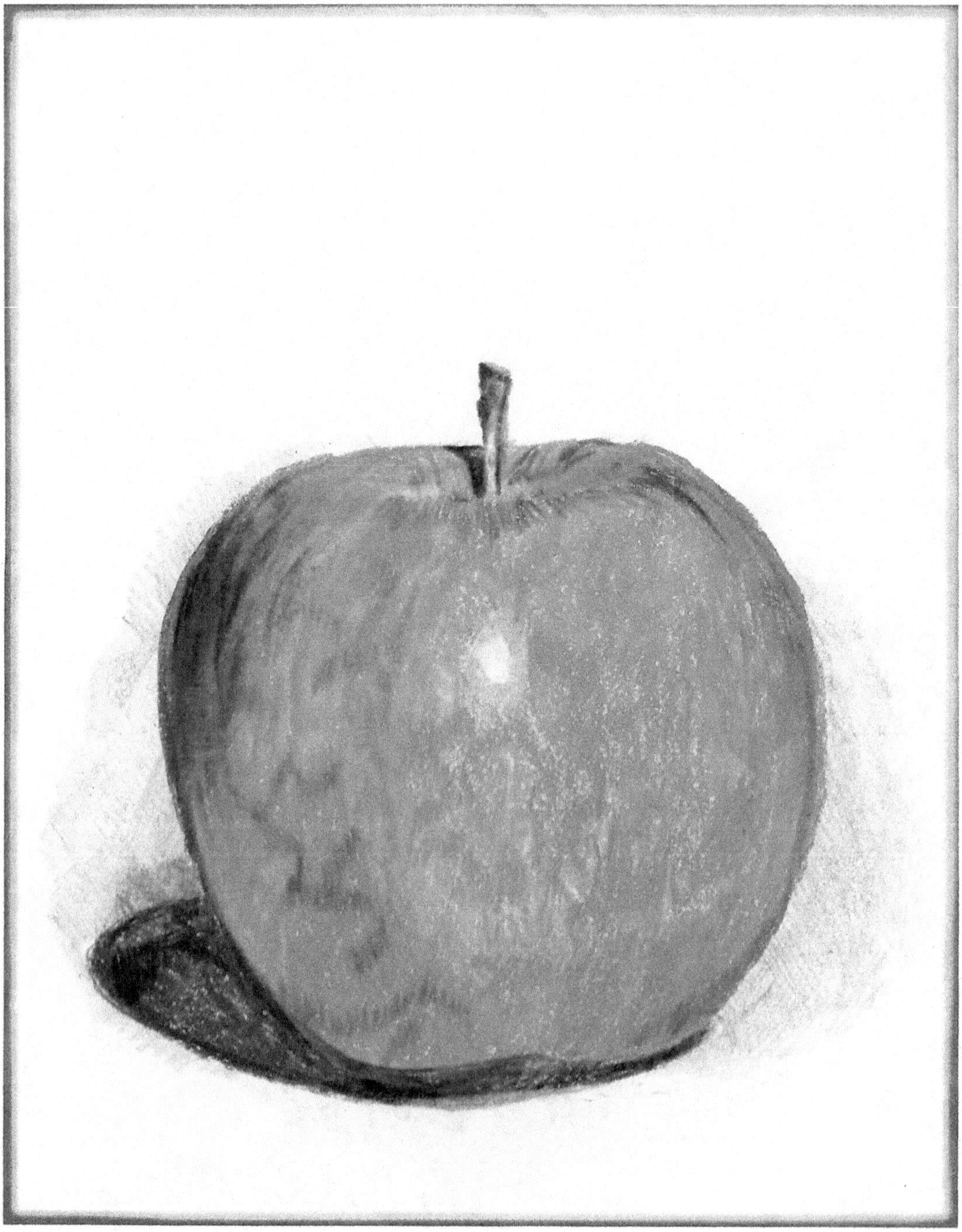

www.ingramcontent.com/pod-product-compliance
Lightning Source LLC
Chambersburg PA
CBHW082151230526
45467CB00043B/2806
* 9 7 8 1 7 1 2 9 3 6 6 3 4 *